Who gets to carve out the narrative of a war and its aftermath? To what end?

"These poems bear witness to war's stain on the human spirit. Doug Rawlings eloquently combines compassion and courage with agony and honesty — an attitude humanity will need to end the tragedy of war, promote a peaceful world, and survive together."

— Paul K. Chappell, an Iraq War veteran, and Peace Leadership Director for the Nuclear Age Peace Foundation. He graduated from West Point in 2002.

"Doug Rawlings' poems about the Vietnam War, full of anger, shame, suffering and solace, are hard to bear —- as they should be. His poems about family life, children, the passing of friends since the war are honest, vulnerable, playful and loving. Together they allow him, and us, full humanity, an expansion of humanity that is particularly poignant in light of its denial to those on both sides who did not survive the war."

— Rob Shetterly, the painter of Americans Who Tell the Truth, a series of portraits honoring the words and work of courageous Americans throughout history.

"Doug Rawlings' courageous and compassionate poetry positions us in front of a mirror and holds us there. We see brutal aggression from the vantage point of the tortured, maimed, bereaved and traumatized people who can't escape the horror. The poems don't aim to mesmerize. Rawlings wants to abolish war."

— Kathy Kelly, American peace activist, pacifist and author, one of the founding members of Voices in the Wilderness, and currently a co-coordinator of Voices for Creative Nonviolence.

"I have met Doug Rawlings only once, and then only in passing at a Veterans for Peace convention in his home state of Maine in 2010, but I have been reading his poetry for nearly 40 years. Spending time with this compilation of his life's work, I feel as if I'm in the company of an old and dear and trusted friend. The range of his emotions, the diversity of his interests, the keenness of his sensibilities, his capacity to be fully and consciously human leave no doubt that his has been and continues to be a life examined and well worth living."

"Orion Rising is a most interesting variety of poems. Some are poignantly 'political' to assure the reader that the 'silences of our fathers will not do' when as ex-soldiers the knowledge of the crimes of our nation deeply disturb our souls; some convey the musings of passion derived from love of family and land experienced in the 'crackling meadows' of rural Maine; and others the joys of a father as he is "wondering out loud" to his children.

"Be prepared to be uncomfortably provoked, but then inspired by the wonders of nature and children, all from the experiences of a genuine long-time Maine resident."

"Doug Rawlings confronts the worst of life, and celebrates the best of life, in poems that transform calcified clichés into lightning bug flashes of insight, foresight and delight. His war poetry punctures the patriotic balloon that imploded amid soldiers in Vietnam. His political poetry turns home front homilies into trumpet calls for peace campaigns. And his poet's gaze on family, friends and nature — from his corner of Maine to the star-spangled universe — is no less, quite often, breath-taking."

Doug Rawlings is a Vietnam War veteran and a founding member of Veterans For Peace.

ORION RISING

COLLECTED POEMS

By
DOUG RAWLINGS

Illustrations
By
Carol Scribner

Cover Art
By
Rob Shetterly

ISBN: 978-1-312-08435-3

DEDICATION

This collection of poems is dedicated to the ones I love, admire, and, in return for the wonder they bring into my life, cherish.

First and foremost, Judy, who met me on my return from the Vietnam War and has been with me ever since. My children, Jen and Josh, who have taught me to stay in the world and never, ever, give up on the possibilities of peace. My son-in-law, David, and my daughter-in-law, Kelly, who have blessed us with their love. Jordan, Xochitl, and Iona, the grandest children a man could possibly have to guide him through this latest generation's travails and joys.

And to my esteemed brothers and sisters who have joined with us to form Veterans For Peace. As a founding member of VFP, I have watched the organization grow into a force to be reckoned with on the world stage. It began in Maine in 1985 and has expanded to include chapters in every state of the union, as well as chapters in England and Vietnam. Our mission is as daunting as it is straightforward — to abolish war. And our means equally so — to do so nonviolently. My deepest gratitude to those who have chosen to take on the most important work a veteran can ever do.

In 1985, the five founders were asked to outline why they took on this task. My statement is below.

Fifteen years ago I survived that latest, crazy forgotten war of ours. And for a long time I was more or less satisfied with that. After all, survival was better than the other alternative I witnessed in Southeast Asia, that some of you witnessed on the six o'clock news, and that our children catch glimpses of in their distorted textbooks. But now I have children of my own. Beautiful, happy children. And I remember the faces of other so-called "survivors": the five year old Vietnamese girls selling their mothers; the ten year old "dump boys" who scrounged for our garbage by day and snaked through our barbed wire by night; and now the faces of Central American children surviving yet another onslaught of our mindless, blood-soaked technology. Survival may have been good enough for me fifteen years ago, but it is not enough for my children — or yours. It is not enough for the children of El Salvador, for the children of Nicaragua, for the children of Honduras, or for the children of Guatemala. It is not enough.

As a veteran, then, I feel a specific obligation to bring back old memories, to rekindle anguish and despair long buried, and to speak out against this military madness that has so grotesquely distorted our past, that is tearing apart our present, and that threatens to extinguish our future. We, as veterans, as survivors, should ask for ...DEMAND... more than survival for the children of the world. We have an obligation to put the true face of the American military machine in full view for all to see. We must insist that we and others educate ourselves about how the military in this country has turned our existence on this planet into one of survival rather than into one of nourishment and compassion for others.

A group such as Veterans For Peace can offer us, veterans of war, a vehicle to bring our special message to the children of the world. Together we can work for a world where there will be no more war memorials. It is the least — and the most — we can do.

                                        Doug Rawlings
                                        Veterans For Peace

ACKNOWLEDGEMENTS

There is something profoundly misleading in the term "self-publishing." Since this collection of poems is not the product of a publishing house, I grant that it does fall into the category of the self-published. Yet there were many "selves" who joined with me to bring this work into the world. Indeed without them these poems would have stayed stashed away in a jumble of notebooks and journals. For all the good these words bring into a reader's life, the following people must be thanked for their invaluable contributions. For all the flaws found within, only the poet himself should stand accused.

JEFF KELLEY, good neighbor and master of the self-publishing world, for his work on formatting the collection

CAROL SCRIBNER, long time good friend and teacher, for her exquisite sketches

ROB SHETTERLY, friend and inspirational peace activist, for his life work and for this book's cover art

DUD HENDRIK, friend and confidant, fellow 'namvet and VFP member, for his wise counsel

TARAK KAUFF AND ELLEN DAVIDSON, much admired peace activists and friends, for their encouragement and wise advice

GRETCHEN LEGLER AND RUTH HILL, long time friends and much-admired writers, for their persistent encouragement

TABLE OF CONTENTS

I. A SURVIVOR'S MANUAL:
OUT OF THE ASHES

II. THE MAINE POEMS:
FAMILY, FRIENDS, AND PLACE

ORION RISING

I. A SURVIVOR'S MANUAL:

OUT OF THE ASHES

I. A SURVIVOR'S MANUAL:
OUT OF THE ASHES

It was in the early 1980's that I came across Robert Bly's *Forty Poems Touching On Recent American History,* (Beacon Press, 1970). Here was what I was looking for, even if I didn't know it at the time — a sort of "poetics" that carefully defines and explains the importance of political poetry. Below are some excerpts from this collection with my own reflections attached.

Bly: "Most educated people advise that poetry on political subjects should not be attempted. For an intricate painting, we are urged to bring forward our finest awareness. At the same time, we understand that we should leave that awareness behind when we go to examine political acts. Our wise men and wise institutions assure us that national political events are beyond the reach of ordinary, or even extraordinary, human sensitivity."

"That habit is not new: Thoreau's friends thought that his writings on nature were very good, but that he was beyond his depth when he protested against the Mexican War...."

Me: as I settled into life here in Maine, and began helping to raise a young family, and continued teaching, I found myself often torn between the demands of my personal life and a mounting anguish over the rampant militarism taking over this country. As a Vietnam war veteran I felt a certain obligation to speak out, using my brief experience in the military, but how? The poems included in this section attempt to bring together my personal journey as a family man with my public journey as a budding peace activist.

Bly: "Most Americans have serious doubts about the morality of the Vietnam War. We are all aware of the large number of spirited and courageous young Americans in the Resistance who are refusing induction and are risking and being given lengthy prison sentences."

"The majority of American draftees, however, go into the Army as they are told. Their doubt is interrupted on its way, and

1

does not continue forward to end in an act.... This failure to carry through means essentially that American culture has succeeded in killing some sensibilities. In order to take the rebellious and responsible action, the (person) thinking must be able to establish firm reasons for it; and in order to imagine those reasons, (her or his) awareness must have grown, over years, finer and finer. The 'invisible organs of government,' schools, broadcasting houses, orthodox churches, move to kill the awareness. The schools emphasize competitiveness over compassion; television and advertising do their part in numbing the sensibilities...."

Me: oh my, these two paragraphs resonate deeply with me. I was drafted out of graduate school (1968), could see the ravages of the Vietnam war in the faces of guys I knew in high school, and of course followed the news somewhat. Yet when my draft notice came, I went (much like Tim O'Brien in his "Rainy River" piece, I was too cowardly to resist). I think one of the forces that drove me into high school English teaching (my initial bachelor's degree is in Economics) was this desire to get into the schools and somehow do some kind of penance while "saving" these kids from taking the misguided path I took. I only lasted seven years as a high school teacher.

Bly: "The calculated effort of a society to kill awareness helps explain why so few citizens take rebellious actions. But I'm not sure it explains why so few American poets have written political poems.... It's clear that many of the events that create our foreign relations and our domestic relations come from more or less hidden impulses in the American psyche.... But if that is so, then the poet's main job is to penetrate that husk around the American psyche, and since that psyche is inside (the poet) too, the writing of political poetry is like the writing of personal poetry, a sudden drive by the poet inward...."

"When a poet succeeds in driving part way inward, he or she often develops new energy that carries her or him on through the polished husk of the inner psyche that deflects most citizens or poets. Once inside the psyche, she or he can speak of inward and political things with the same assurance...."

"The life of the nation can be imagined also not as something deep inside our psyche, but as a psyche larger than the psyche of anyone living, a larger sphere, floating above everyone. In order for the poet to write a true political poem, he or she has to be able to have such a grasp of her or his own concerns that he or she can leave them for a while, and then leap up into this other psyche...."

Me: I kind of sensed this phenomenon but really couldn't articulate it until after I read Bly. Aha! There is a connection between the inner workings of a child, a partner, a veteran, and a government run amok.

Bly: "Some poets try to write political poems impelled by hatred, or fear. But these emotions are heavy, they affect the gravity of the body. What the poet needs to get up that far and bring back something are great leaps of the imagination."

"A true political poem is a quarrel with ourselves, and the rhetoric is as harmful in that sort of poem as in the personal poem. The true political poem does not order us either to take any specific acts: like the personal poem, it moves to deepen awareness...."

Me: indeed. There are pages and pages of diatribe in my journals and workbooks that are weighted down by hatred and rage. They will never see the light of day. However, I do believe that real anger is a legitimate galvanizing force behind some poems. As long as the anger is directed outwards. Many Vietnam war veterans, in my opinion, became self-consumed with anger turned inwards when they came to the realization that they had been duped, used by the government, to give a good part of their lives to an immoral, unjust, and downright stupid war. I admit to dipping into that well of despair, but somehow I have found the resources to resurface again and again. The quarrel that ate me up (eats me up) rambles through my notebooks and, if I am lucky, on occasion is allowed to spring free into more useful, universal musings, into poems.

Bly: "The new critical influence in poetry began to dim in the middle 1950's, just at the time Americans' fantastic capacity for aggression and self-delusion began to be palpable like rising water to the beach walker....."

Me: I just had to include this final comment from one of this country's finest poets and, in his own way, strongest activists. His work calls to mind a favorite Bertolt Brecht statement: "Art is not a mirror held up to reality, but a hammer with which to shape it." It is my firm belief that those of us who have served in war have an obligation to speak of the "aggression" that we have witnessed and participated in, while hammering away at this debilitating self-delusion.

So I found some kind of comfort, if not inspiration, from Bly's insistence that poems can be written that would "penetrate deeply into the psyche of the nation" without sacrificing a personal voice.

ON WAR MEMORIALS

Corporate America
be forewarned:
We* are your karma
We are your Orion
rising in the night sky
We are the scorpion
in your jackboot

Corporate America
be forewarned:
We will not buy
your bloody parades anymore
We refuse your worthless praise
We spit on
your war memorials

Corporate America
be forewarned:
We will not feed you
our bodies
our minds
our children
anymore

Corporate America
be forewarned:
If we have our way
(and we will)
the real war memorials
will rise
from your ashes

* *American Vietnam War veterans "... who refused to honor
America's longest war." —-from the introduction to the anthology*
Demilitarized Zones (1976)

THE WALL
To Jerry Genesio, the founder of Veterans For Peace

Descending into this declivity
dug into our nation's capitol
by the cloven hoof
of yet another one of our country's
tropical wars

Slipping past the names of those
whose wounds
refuse to heal

Slipping past the panel where
my name would have been
could have been
perhaps should have been

Down to The Wall's greatest depth
where the beginning meets the end
I kneel

Staring through my own reflection
beyond the names of those
who died so young

Knowing now that The Wall
has finally found me –
58,000 thousand-yard stares
have fixed on me
as if I were their Pole Star
as if I could guide their mute testimony
back into the world
as if I could connect all those dots
in the nighttime sky

As if I
could tell them
the reason why

NUMBER 7

I was a
Good Humor Man.
Lost my job
Got drafted

I can never
go back again
Lost my
Good Humor
Lost $80.00 a week
Can never
Have it again

You gain
Goodwill
being a Good Humor
Man.
You establish a route
You make friends

I lost them all:
My bike my cart
my bell
are all gone now
My smile too.
All my friends
    cried
on the Last Day.

On the Last Day
I gave all my
ice cream away
        Free
to all my friends
They still cried.
I did too

Came Home with
an Empty Cart
and my Boss said
        "Good
            All sold."
I said
        "No All Free."
And cried.

He didn't cry.
He said
        "You owe me $16.00."

I think his brother
works at my Draft Board.

LEAVING THE INDUCTION CENTER

We were now
all riders
on those olive drab
government buses

trying to make some sense
out of this thing
they called military justice

Still a bunch
of minors
digging about
in our own little ruins

Burrowing through
the dangerous trash
of our own silly illusions

We were all of us
just drifters
caught up in
a dirty little war

Left to ride it out
alone on our own
thin little prayers

MEDIC

medic medic
if you can
come help me
wash this blood
from off my hands

come pour cologne
on this stink
give this rotting breath
some
eternal listerine

come stop his screams
from tearing through
my dreams
my dreams

come help me
file it all away
pilate it all away
on an airplane

going home

YOU SHOULD WRITE ABOUT IT

You should
write a book
about it.
Like the time
you held
that hand
or when the stars
burst into flares
Or how about when
the earth flew away
before your eyes?

And how about
that smell?

Maybe you should write
a manual
detailing how to
burn your shit
in diesel fuel
before breakfast.

Or maybe you
could write a song
about the 175's
and the 8-inchers
blowing away your eardrums.
Or perhaps a poem
to the girls
in their wooden faces
making love to the moon
bouncing behind your
shoulder.

Well, how about it?
It's been awhile.
I know you still got it
in you.
Write something
anything
god damn you

It won't kill you, you know.
At least not anymore than
it already has.

KIA

A TELEGRAM TO RICHARD NIXON

If he was killed in action
then tell me in what act.

What was he doing
when time stood still?

Tell me anything
save that he was intent upon
killing another

for the likes of you.

AO

*To Paul Reuterschan who died from
exposure to Agent Orange*

It blooms
It blossoms
It softly implodes

It kneads me like dough

It eats me whole

It killed me in `nam
forty years ago.

SURVIVOR'S MANUAL

To Judy

If your arms and legs
are still intact
you are a survivor

If tall meadow grasses
still delight you with
their sudden pheasants
you are a survivor

If the faces of passing children
remain the faces
of passing children
you are a survivor

If your nightmares
will wait for the night
you are a survivor

If you can find your way
back into someone's love
you, my friend, are a survivor

A SOLDIER'S LAMENT

They came every day
to sit
beneath the barbed wire

They came to sell us
what they would:
a comb
a ring
a sister
      if they could

They came to torture us
these children of the dust
with their eyes
with their lies
the ice in their smiles

To torture us
with their lives

They came and now
they will not leave

They came and now
our souls
blister and burn
across the years
above the bonfires
of children's curses

BICENTENNIAL POEM: AUTUMN 1976

She is two now
and can almost
speak in sentences
Why, if this were seven years ago
and she Vietnamese,

She would almost
be old enough
to sell her mother

WHEEL DREAMS

"If in some smothering dreams, you too could pace
Behind the wagon that we flung him in,
And watch the white eyes writhing in his face"
— Wilfred Owen*

Each night of the full moon
my dreams reinvent
Wilfred Owen's wagon wheel
only to hoist it up
forged anew
above the fairgrounds

carrying our ripest youth
over the carnival
and into the night air
where fingering the stars
and devouring the lusty fireworks
they never fail to feel
too late

the ferris wheel turning
to drop them off
one by one
into some jungle

where the meat wheel
squeals
in delight

a buzz saw
working its way
through green pine
devouring the moon
oiling its teeth

on their succulent pleas

* As a World War I combatant, Owen witnessed his fellow soldiers choking to death on mustard gas. Victims were thrown onto the back of horse drawn wagons, which the survivors trudged behind.

15

FORMULA FOR A SINGLE CAR SUICIDE
(A TRIED AND TRUE VETERAN'S WAY OUT)

Take a lonely country road.
Choose a tree (most any one will do).
Go for it like a bat out of the hell
they have put together just for you.
Take that iron body bag
and wrap it around you good and tight.
Go ahead and break the sound barrier
with your skull.

You don't have to take any of their shit anymore.
Now that you have finally
come home
from the war.

FLASHBACK
"...stare upon the ash of all I burned."
— *Wilfred Owen*

Suddenly
the ash catches,
bursting into
betel-mouthed mamasans
licking at
that open sore
in my dreams
nibbling at
the scars
of what I once was
what I thought I buried
long ago

their searching tongues
plunging into that one special wound

the only one
that can ignite
once again

the spirit
of the bayonet:

"Kill, kill, kill.
Have no mercy.
Kill."

CONTEMPLATING SUICIDE:
A VETERAN'S NOTE

I stand astride
a deep narrow canyon
its walls the black that
nullifies all light
that disallows reflection

At the bottom
of the canyon
squirms a stream
still cutting away
after more than four decades

When the time does come
to dive down
on to the river's edge
I will do so gladly

if only to be free
of those whose screams
have heralded so long
my unfortunate survival

TO THE GRADUATING CLASS OF 1993

If they got you thinking about
signing up
just to kill you some time
(since nothing else is going down)
you better be getting ready
to kill you
some women
and some children too

and you better be getting ready
to kill you
some time
doing time
doing some long time
locked up
in their screams

PTSD REMEDIES

For Tarak Kauff

First off, drop the "P"
There's nothing "post"
about a mirror that threatens
to slit your wrist

But keep the "D"
I'll take "disorder" – sweet chaos –
any time over this close order drill
that haunts my early morning hours

Then let the healing begin:

(1) Ask yourself: "Who am I?"

(2) Ask your lover: "Who are you?"

(3) Remain still. Wait for he or she
to whisper: "Who are we?"

Now the ache
has permission to leave

and the sunrise
can ease you into
another day

DEATH OF A FRIEND

his death
struck my soul
as a fish
strikes a line
driven by some madness
    to leap at shining steel

his death
struck my soul
as a kite
in the wind
    yearning to be free

his death
begs me to follow
pulls me toward him
my hands grow weak
and
    cannot break
    the string

GOVERNMENT ISSUE

The young man
flashes by
wheel on wheel
sparkling in the sun

2 dead fish lie
before him
neatly pressed
in denim

GOVERNMENT ISSUE AT THE V.A. HOSPITAL

the pale green doors
remained mute before him

he read "Freight Elevator"
thought he was in the wrong place

thought again
and knew he got it right

what was left of his family
waited downstairs
in the lobby
for what was left

of him

THE DOW LEGACY

Eleven million gallons of Agent Orange were sprayed on 5 million acres of Vietnam from 1962 to 1970. Dow Chemical was a major supplier of Agent Orange.

The seed that your
malicious wizardry
planted in me on the banks
of the Bong Son River
may now be bearing fruit
in my own children —
innocent passengers
on your agent orange special
heavy with your brainchild
festering
in their genes.

MAINLINE QUATRAINS

the shadow of a man glides down the road
dressed in dust wrapped in grays
bent earthward beneath an invisible load
moving silently through his endless days

alone in the night sitting in his rented room
searching his arm for a heavenly vein
placing his soul on a silver spoon
finding his religion in the candle's flame

his prayers throb to the beat of his blood
his wounds scream for their pinch of salt
his body sways and flows with the flood
he plunges into the deepening vault

VETERANS DAY: 1993*

Why this particular memory
that always comes for me
from a world
a half a world away

With its distinctive rhythms
and its telling rhymes
so different from
the silences
of the incandescent tamaracks
of the oaks and maples blackened
in this soft November rain

If not to join me
in ghoulish adagio
with the gutted deer
swinging in the door yard
with shards of pumpkin skulls
glistening in the village streets

If not to remind me
we are never
that far away from
a time
and a place
where no one
is entirely sane

*After living in a small Maine village for a number of years, I noticed a strange confluence: Veterans Day, Halloween, and deer hunting season come around about the same time. This time of year some of us take notice of the weirdest alliances.

CORDWOOD

"The energy, the faith, the devotion which we bring to
this endeavor will light our country and all who serve it —
and the glow from that fire can truly light the world"
—*from JFK's Inaugural Address*
(20 January 1961)

Late September.
It has been three decades
of oak, maple, ash
the dreaded birch
and elm
cut
split,
stacked
and stacked again

Meanwhile
over at Togus*
my thorazine brothers
tend to their own fall chores
shuffling through twenty years
of smoke and mirrors:

the smoke from JFK's
watchfires
nothing more than
sawed off barrels of burning
shit
the mirrors
beckon
threaten
to slit a wrist

Late September again.
Full moon

Back to the woodpile
to work up a sweat

to clear my head
(fires are burning within fires)

to hold out against
the coming of another
winter's long night

Togus is Maine's Veterans Administration Hospital

23

GIVING SILENCE

For Josh and David turning thirteen

If 'namvets were
ancient shamans
now would be
the moment
we'd choose
to give you
shelter
from the coming storm.

But we are merely
survivors
of suburbs and cities
not forest nor mountain
modern men
offering you
our silences
our words
to guide you
going out
on your own.

Yet we have known
for years now
that the silences
of our fathers
will not do.
And we have found
that words alone
cannot be
the sacred knives
you need
to bleed you free
of your
raging doubts.

So listen up
to what we have found
between our own silences:
Open up your fists
Watch women move
Scorn uniforms
Don't march
Dance

PROMETHEUS AGAIN

To The Men of the 7/15th Artillery
Bong Son, Vietnam

We once
brought
fire
down
on some village
children
in that latest
crazy
forgotten war
of ours.

Now we have
come home
to spend
our days
asleep
on park benches
beneath
corporate
newspapers
of indifference

and
our nights
chained to their
trash cans, drunk
on their
Ripple, muscatel,
Thunderbird,

retching our guts up
into their blind and
relentless
dawn.

NARCISSUS AGAIN

Picture
William Westmoreland
kneeling in a meadow
filling fast oh fast
with flakes of
white phosphorous

And he —
gazing at his own face
reflected in pools of
jellied flesh —
he
tries to rise

but his arms can only flail
at the orange sky
and his fingers ripple off
into spidery filaments
of yellow smoke

And it is now —
and it will be now forever —
that William Westmoreland
feels the faces
of Vietnamese peasants
melting into anguished oblivion

SISYPHUS AGAIN

Picture
Richard Nixon
in loin cloth
and Ho Chi Minh slicks
dragging
a block of stone
to the top
of some ancient temple
deep beneath Cambodian
triple canopy

stumbling back
to his jungle home
for a bowl of rancid rice
for a night of troubled sleep

springing awake
near dawn
feeling B-52's
walk their load
toward his new home

Picture
poor Richard Nixon
his stone
toppling to his feet
beginning
another day's
eternal work

COMMENTS ON THE DMZ POEMS

"Number 7" *(page 7)*
"Medic" *(page 9)*
"A Soldier's Lament" *(page 13)*
"Death of a Friend" *(page 19)*
"Mainline Quatrains" *(page 21)*
"Sunset: Thoreau Falls" *(page 43)*
"Jen" *(page 94)*

These seven poems were my initial attempts to use verse as a way to make sense of my world. They were included in a 1976 anthology of Vietnam veterans' poetry published by East River Anthology Press (editors Jan Barry and W.D. Ehrhart).

I served in the 7/15th artillery from July of 1969 to August of 1970 in the Central Highlands of Vietnam. At the time of publication I was living in Bath, Maine with Judy, Jen, my daughter, and Josh, my son. I was teaching high school English.

The editors begin the collection with this inscription from "The Odyssey":

> "Odysseus," Achilles rejoined:
> "Spare me your honor of heroic death.
> Put me on earth again, and I would rather be
> a servant in a poor man's house
> than king of all these dead..."

They then dedicate the anthology to "...those who refused to honor America's longest war."

Their introduction reads, in part:

"This book is not about Vietnam. It is about America. Survivors of the Indochina tragedy returned like no other American war veterans. We came back alone, one at a time, day after day, for fifteen years. The early veterans came back from a land few Americans had ever heard of. The last veterans came back from a land few Americans want to remember. Almost all of us came back to a homeland which bore little resemblance to the one we left — not because it had changed, but because we had.

Bicentennial America is scrambling hard to erase Vietnam from its memory and its conscience. But try as it will, official

America cannot so easily erase its Vietnam veterans. There are 3,000,000 of us. We touch the lives of millions more....(And) we often joined our generation ... to stop the insanity in Indochina created by our own government.

For over a decade 'Vietnam' was a high-voltage wire running through every part of America, a state of mind as well as an Asian state. Many Americans came to feel, along with those of us who directly experienced the fire, that they too were veterans of the Indochina war....

If the poems in our predecessor volume, *Winning Hearts And Minds: War Poems by Vietnam Veterans*, were written out of fire — and indeed they were — these works are written out of the ashes. One day, perhaps, lotus will grow in places where the fire once burned.

Poems and prose poetry, art and photography, *Demilitarized Zones: Veterans After Vietnam* is a collection of letters to America. And to all human beings on this our only earth."

BOAT PEOPLE

1.

lambs
descendant
from
the latest
slaughter
come ashore
tugging the war
behind them
and we finally
show some concern:

can a sapper
really hotwire
our daughters?

2.

no need
to worry
though:
we're in America
where we've
weathered
napalmed faces
and
apple-cheeked
junkies
before.

We know
we are secure.

After all, the six o'clock news
will lose them too.

HOW TO PREVENT NUCLEAR WAR

"We have not inherited the earth from our ancestors; we have borrowed it from our descendants"
— a Native American proverb

Give to each president
each prime minister
each admiral
each general an acorn

Tell them to plant it
where they'll never see it again

Tell them not to
think about it

Rather, each morning
before thoughts crowd in
tell them to
feel it

To feel its roots
stretching into the earth

To feel it aching
toward the sun

To feel it breathing
into the wind

Tell them to feel it
swinging
with the laughter
of their children's
children

KRISTALLNACHT REVISITED

snug we'll be
tucked away in our
little technoghettoes
for the night
when the mushroom clouds
begin their march
up the coast

and then how we will cower
in our corners
until the firestorm
pounds down our doors

until we are torn loose
by the black leather gloves
of our calculated ignorance

until we are thrust headlong
into the blast furnace
exploding down the street

where the corner store
used to be

HIROSHIMA SKAT

you rode in on
your mandrake root
sticking your bloody thumb
in to their karmic soup
dripping your bloody fire
in to their autumn air

but then you said
they wouldn't care

besides
how would they look
strolling down the street
swaying and colliding
with no hair
with skin slopping
into puddles
at their feet
with eyes baked
into custard
melting out
into their streets?

besides
where could they have gone
in that heat
with no hair?

Nowhere.

IN THE AMERICAN VEIN

*for Charlie Clements**

El Salvador's not Vietnam
San Salvador's not Saigon
yet something seems
to have slid away
into the South China Sea

to be born again
in El Salvador

Seems something's
down there
dancing once again
to the staccato rhythm
of the M-16 on rock and roll
to the shimmering whine
of the 175's coming in low

Seems something's
down there
hungering
for the American vein
once again

Seems something's
fixing to shoot up
whatever youth it can find

to do up major death

not in Vietnam
not in Saigon
but in El Salvador
in San Salvador

this trip around
the melting clock
of America

killing time

Charlie Clements is a Vietnam War veteran who refused to fly combat missions into Cambodia. For that he was given the "Catch 22 treatment." After leaving the service, he became a medical doctor, working with refugees in southern California and there became aware of the plight of El Salvadorans fighting against U.S. supported tyrants. He spent a year in the jungles of El Salvador providing medical services for the FMLN.

34

LOW INTENSITY WARFARE

Up here
we're working up
this winter's wood
Down there
below the Rio
below the Durangoes
in the fruit section
of our global IGA
deep in the sweet underbelly
of America
Down there
we're stacking up
bodies

Up here
fall is in the air
the mornings are crisp and clear
the leaves die beautifully
in earth browns
translucent yellows
blood reds
Down there
young peasants
are slipping into puddles
of mangled skin
Down there
Willie Peter*
is hard at work
Down there
the morning air
smells of burning flesh

Up here
business
is as usual.

* "Willie Peter" is army slang for white phosphorous

HANDS

I come in from doing wood
this late November evening
catch my gloves
out of the corner of an eye
clutching and aching
drying beneath the stove

Picture the hands
of Victor Jara*
lopped off by my tax dollars
scrambling like headless chickens
across the stadium floor

Think of my own hands
where they have been
what they have done
in the service of corporate goons

Go to the bathroom sink
wash them before supper
think I see Pontius Pilate
in the mirror
staring back at me

*Victor Jara was a Chilean teacher, theatre director, poet, singer-songwriter, and a strong political activist. He started to work in the service of Unidad Popular's electoral campaign in 1970. He became the cultural ambassador of Salvador Allende's government, organizing song tours all over Latin America. In 1973 he sang during programs reserved against fascism and civil war on national TV.

On the morning of September 12, Victor Jara was taken, along with thousands of others, as a prisoner to the Estadio Chile (renamed the Estadio Victor Jara 2003). In the hours and days that followed, many of those detained in the stadium were tortured and killed there by the military forces. Jara was repeatedly beaten and tortured; the bones in his hands were broken as were his ribs. His last moments had become famous through testimonies of other political prisoners who said that his captors mockingly suggested that he play guitar for them as he lay on the ground with broken hands. Defiantly, he sang part of "Venceremos" (We Will Win), a song supporting the Unidad Popular party.

COUNTER-RECRUITMENT WORK
MT. BLUE HIGH SCHOOL 2003

We face off:
the recruiter
some Hispanic kid
in cammies
from the Bronx

stuck up here in this very
white farming town

me
paunchy, balding, weary-eyed
three decades removed
from my own war

Both of us
homing in on
these high school kids
not slick enough to get out of town
on their own

He needs them to make his rank

I need them to help me
stay sane

God
if you're still around
damn
this fucking war

ON THE WAR IN IRAQ

On this September day in 2007
on this day of bright sky blue
of tree lines splattered
in red yellow orange and green
I am as old as my father was in 1969 —
my year in Vietnam —
he caught between dread
and a morbid curiosity,
taking in the six o'clock news

Now I see what he must have seen
watching the ticker tape
scrolling across the bottom
of his hopeless little screen:

soldiers dying two by two
three by three
always alone,

keeping half an eye open
for his youngest son

Now I wonder what I really knew
four decades ago, and I wonder
what I can know
or pretend to know
of today's soldiers
of their pain
their fear of not
coming home
completely sane

Though of course I know
that is an impossibility —
coming home all of one piece —
knowing now
what they know
of what
I knew
of war
and its utter disregard
for your sanity

MEMO TO THE PENTAGON

Dedicated to the Veterans Peace Teams, wherever you are....

We are works in progress, you know.

Thought you had us in Basic,
didn't you?
Thought you froze our spirits
to your bayonets,
didn't you?

Thought we'd stay your
racist robots
lost in your war zones
for life,
didn't you?

Thought maybe we'd do
the VA Thorazine shuffle
for the rest of our lives,
didn't you?

Guess what?
Wrong again.
We got our
ghost shirts on,
and we're coming
for you

Sure, we got
a long way to go

But don't look now —
you don't.

GUANTANAMO POEM JANUARY 2014

Egypt Pond, Maine
Second Poem For the Veterans Peace Teams,
wherever they are

It is legal, you know
The state even grants permits
Of course there are limits
And you do need the landowner's permission

Here's how he does it up in Maine:

He cuts a good sized sapling
Then he augurs a hole through the ice
Sticks the steel trap on to one end
And lowers it to the pond floor

The beaver swims over out of curiosity, I suppose,
And ends up with a leg opened to the bone
Her efforts to break free are futile
She is pinned down, drowns (they have lungs, you know)

Same, same in Guantanamo
Tie the poor bastards down
Let them feel what it's like to drown
Do it again and again

What to do?

Up here I strap on skates
Take to the pond under cover of the stars
Find the saplings and shake them up and down
Maybe spring the traps, I don't know

You guys, our brave brothers and sisters,
Wrap yourselves in prison orange
Fast for days on end, gather at the White House fence
Maybe change some minds, we just don't know

But I won't quit and neither will you
After all, all of us, no matter who we are
We all need each other to be free
For all of us, all of us, to breathe

"We all need each other to be free
For all of us, all of us, to breathe"

MEMO TO AMERICA

DATE: 12/29/2010
FROM:THE PENTAGON
RE: GET SOME SLEEP & REST IN PEACE

Last night
Palestinian
Afghani
Iraqi
children
women
men
died
in
your sleep

Shhhh.

Don't get up

EMERGENCY EXIT

In case of an emergency
(i.e., war)
(i.e., preparation for war)
(i.e., life in 21st century North America)
Do not use the legislative process.
Take the streets.

SUNSET: THOREAU FALLS

I hear nothing
but the falls
see nothing
but the mountain
across the valley

Time hangs here
like moss
patiently devouring
the tree
splitting the rock
dimming the eye

The scent of pine
is on my hands
the sun dances
off the falls
into a thousand needles
of soaring light

The ominous shadow
of the mountain
crawls toward us
pulling the sky down
in a flurry of colors

ORION RISING

II. THE MAINE POEMS:

FAMILY, FRIENDS, AND PLACE

II. THE MAINE POEMS: FAMILY, FRIENDS, AND PLACE

Mary Oliver closes her "manual," *A Poetry Handbook*, (Harcourt, 1994) by referencing Ralph Waldo Emerson — "The poem is a confession of faith" — and then riffing on that notion:

> "Which is to say, the poem is not an exercise. It is not 'wordplay.' Whatever skill, or beauty it has, it contains something beyond language devices, and has a purpose other than itself. And it is part of the sensibility of the writer. I don't mean in any 'confessional' way, but that it reflects from the writer's point of view — his or her perspective — out of all the sum of his or her experience."

> "Athletes take care of their bodies. Writers must similarly take care of the sensibility that houses the possibility of poems. There is nourishment in books, other art, history, philosophies — in holiness and in mirth. It is in honest hands-on labor also; I don't mean to indicate a preference for the scholarly life. And it is in the green world — among people, and animals, and trees for that matter, if one genuinely cares about trees. A mind that is lively and inquiring, compassionate, curious, angry, full of music, full of feeling, is a mind full of possible poetry. Poetry is a life-cherishing force. And it requires a vision — a faith, to use an old-fashioned term. Yes, indeed. For poems are not words, after all, but fires for the cold, ropes let down to the lost, something as necessary as bread in the pockets of the hungry. Yes, indeed."

Me: All of the following poems were written in a Maine farmhouse built in the early 1820's. It is a house surrounded by meadows and woods and, close by, a 60 acre pond. When clear, which it mostly is, the night sky either aches with stars and stars, or glows with the moon. Orion dances for us especially brilliantly in the dead of winter.

For almost forty years we have heated with wood — sometimes up to ten cords a year. We also maintain organic gardens and have just built a large greenhouse. No matter what other jobs we have taken on to survive here, we could never escape the hold that the house and the land have had over us. And, to be frank, we never really want to.

So it is a life of books and "hands-on" labor that infuse many of the poems in this section. It is no mistake that love of the land, melded with love of family and friends, weaves throughout them.

HOMAGE TO THE WINTER MOON

Apple trees
stripped of their summer fruit
squat
like ancient mothers
fingering the intricate lacework
of their own moon shadows

And we
slipping into their solemn world
feel the evening's strident headlines
grow silent

As the peace of this place
of this moment
sifts down into us
drifts into its own elaborate design
builds deep within us
its own magical pillars

to carry us through
the days ahead

BACK FLOATING ON RANGELEY LAKE

skin stretched
between stars
and lake stone

a tympanum
of protoplasm
food for the mosquito
(eaten by the leaping trout)

while the me
that is rarely seen
floats out and away

humbled for a moment
by its place
in this great
food chain

GEORGE SOPER — A FARMER – DYING

George sat
in the kitchen's slanting light
watching one last Winter
give in to Spring

the snow opening to
patches of meadow

the tumescent frost
breaking ground

for the planting
of his flesh

BLIZZARD

the pear tree
stands alone
as if a character
in the corner
of some Zen scroll

all else
under the weather

JOSH TURNING ONE

He sits and stares
into the mirror
stoical as the heron
at the water's edge

and, as that great bird,
stirred out of his reverie,
breaks the still water
with his flight

so shall he, dear son,
mark his path
through my life

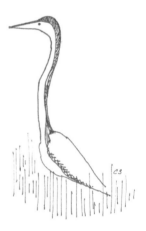

TO JOSH TURNING SIX

1.
The loon fishing
quietly swallows itself
into the lake
leaving no trace

2.
Going simple
you have now
more than you will
ever need to use

3.
The morning rain gathers
onto the apple bud
only to fall
of its own weight

4.
Going clear
knowing you gain
exactly what you need
to lose

50

DAEDALUS AGAIN

Me: I'm the driver
the one with the prehensile thumbs
and all the wisdom
needed to guide these 2000 pounds of rolled steel
through the night
dodging the wandering farm cat, porcupine, skunk

You, son: you're the chosen one
captive in the dash light's subterranean glow
finger punching the radio
in search of some dj savvy enough
to stroke the pain out of your pulsing rage

Me: I'm still trying to figure us out
wondering if after these seventeen years
I'm any closer to you
than I was when I caressed your mother's swollen belly
intent even then on tracing out designs
to carry us both beyond the hopeless maze
I have made of my own journey

You, son: I can't blame for collapsing
into an inertia of your own choosing
moved by instinct
to ward off any warped calculus
any feeble construct
fashioned from these clumsy thumbs
this superfluous wisdom

FATHER GRIEVING

Midnight
The house sleeps
Your son in bed pissed at you
for what you've done not done
said
not said
for who you are
for who you aren't
for who knows what

So you head to the john
Look in the mirror
Snatch a towel and bury your face
Cloak gasping tears
Muffle the howl
of inadequacy

You finish
Climb the stairs to bed
Your wife offers you her back
You lie there
supine
unforgiven

You drift off to sleep
having protected
once again
the silence
of your house sleeping

TO JEN TURNING SIXTEEN

" A nameless patient spider...
launched forth filament,
*   filament, filament out of itself...."*
*   — Walt Whitman*

The princess I made you out to be
for all these years
was merely a father's playful fantasy
for which
I do not apologize

Yet celebrating you on this day
A new rider on the rhythm of the moon
I must also mourn my own passing
before your eyes

And take what little comfort
I can
as a father and as a man
trapped in this bittersweet dance:

you spinning out the gossamer threads
of a woman becoming the light
in another man's eyes

THE EXCHANGE
To Sandy F.

You carried your death
closer to the heart than most of us do
(I've been told)
so I guess it wasn't much of a surprise
to some
when they finally collided

But it was to me

And then a card from your wife
She wrote how the poem
to my daughter made you cry
How you sent it off to your own Elizabeth

And I thought:
I've got to meet this guy

And then you died

So now I'm left with this:
I imagine your daughter
reading my poem aloud
the moment of your last breath
knowing through my words
what one father's love
can mean

And you
in exchange
sent forth filaments
of your own exploding heart
deep into my daughter's dreams
fashioning them into a vision
of my death
so intense
that she came downstairs
the next morning
to offer me a smile:
the first we've shared in days

JEN'S WEDDING SONG

Dancing through crackling meadows
Scaring up summertime fireflies
You were born to chase down barn swallows
Stitching up the evening sky

Oh, the birch splits its bark
And the snake its skin
And the child she leaps into the woman
She always has been

Always one to swim against the incoming tide
Or a wildflower aching to bloom
You were born to hitch yourself a ride
On the driving rhythm of the moon

Oh, nothing is really changing
While nothing stays the same
The girls they keep on turning
Into the women they always have been

Following your heart home once again
Sure as Orion rising over Egypt Pond
You were born to make a life of your own
Joining the loons in crazy midnight song

Oh, the birch splits its bark
And the snake its skin
And the child she leaps into the woman
She always has been
Oh, nothing is really changing
While nothing stays the same
Girls they keep on turning
Into the women they always have been

And the girls they keep on turning
Into the women they always have been

VASECTOMY

my semen was
turned to dust today
my vas deferens
knotted into snagged
fishing line

my sperm
detoured
rerouted
turned back onto
themselves
like a mob caught in
a sudden storm
crazed, stomping, strangling
smothering one another
as I sleep
unaware of the death
swirling inside of me

a cry tugs me awake
and, feeling like a eunuch
at the harem door,
I linger at the children's room
listening to the soothing
oasis of their restless sleep

NOON SKIING

crossing my trail
tracks of deer moose
mouse ruffed grouse
snowshoe hare

tracks that follow
our trail
use it for a moment
run with it
then suddenly off
into the woods
to places I'll never be

I stop on the ridge
deep perfect blue sky
catching my breath

and think:
just like the kids

A POEM FOR MY FATHER

"Suddenly I realize that if
I stepped out of my body
I would break into blossom"
— James Wright

My father stretches out before me
his lounge chair coffin off-white polyester
his ersatz death mask snoring softly
his fingers stumbling across his stomach
through the memory of some Chopin etude

It is a mid-afternoon in early July
a thunderstorm is blowing in from off
West Palm Beach
raking the lagoon
sending the mourning doves
back into the trees

I love you, I whisper
loud enough to pull him to the surface
He eyes me startled and scared
his breath catching on something he heard
something that may have been important

We exchange shy smiles
do not speak
I turn back to my reading
he to some meadow of the soul

where old men practice
the silent art
of breaking into blossom

ON BATHING MY MOTHER

This most unnatural of duties repulses us:
You eighty-three my mother
squatting naked
Me reluctantly passing washcloth and soap
over and through this flaccid montage
of skin and muscle
gone to seed.

Then you suddenly laugh, sigh:
"I never thought it would come to this...."

Your words pouring light down on the two of us
and finally I see your body for the temple it is
Hear your laughter as the temple bell
calling me forth
to worship

DISCOVERY

Copernicus
could not have been
more terrified
than our country kids
caught up on
this crowded city street

catching first glimpse
of their place
in the grand scheme
of things
far from the hub
of this madly careening
wheel

ON LEARNING OF THE DEATH OF
MARK BARTHOLOMEW,
A COLLEAGUE

It seems that each Spring
just when I gather the apple leaves
into a tight, neat circle on the lawn
the wind will rise out of the west
quicken and scatter my morning's work

Or just when the snow finally melts
from the meadows and the days of April
begin to lengthen and the frost eases up
and the fiddleheads sprout along the stone wall
to challenge the cold grays of Winter
the basement fills with water

It is good that I learned long ago
to cease forcing answers from the workings of this world
to listen, instead, for the counterweights
that will surely fall into place
to balance even this ache that has found its way
into everything I have done these past six days

Mark, I will learn to not look for your quick laugh
your shy sideways smile
as I pass by the rooms where you taught
but to leave open a space within
for your spirit to seize me with a grip
as sure as your infamous hold on a coffee cup
as true as your damnable ease filling an inside straight

And then I will know
that you have found me again
that you have given us your own life
as a gift that will always move
and that I shall have to do my part
to keep it alive
to meet the despair of this world
with a force of love and hope and wonder
made stronger from having known you

FOR GRETCHEN* TURNING FIFTY
11/24/2010

1.
Carmen launches into her triumphant aria
Bizet moves through you like satin and silk
the crowd sits spellbound
"L'amour est un oiseaux rebelle."

2.
The tree stand shifts slightly
tessellated leaves gather in the morning air
Orion descends. Sunbeams creep through the trees.
Your breath becomes the dew and is gone.

3.
Aracaunas, Wyandottes, and various reds
rising up from their straw nests
pay homage to your amateur chortling
by giving up their new born into your warm hands

4.
Six hundred moons have slipped on by
We of your species celebrate your life with song
while the deer bark out: "l'amour, l'amour, l'amour"
and the barnyard ladies chuckle merrily along

Gretchen is an opera aficionada, a deer hunter, an accomplished essayist, and a raiser of chickens and goats and vegetables.

TO CAROL: MY CHILDREN'S TEACHER

And the moon
Could be a wise fisherwoman
Hauling her jeweled net
Through our seas

And you too
Could be of the moon
Having pulled your tender web
Through my son and daughter
These past five years

And as the sea
Following the moon
Forms the shore
So have you come
Through them
To shape me

FRAGMENTS

Winter quiet farmhouse
midnight
mice in the walls

In the kitchen deep night
deaf to the roar
of the aging refrigerator
then it stops

Cutting through space
trying not to get time
all over my face

Clear thought as wind
no beginning no end
polishing Now into lens

TO JUDY, PREGNANT

little she/he
scratching in your tummy
a kitten
at a half-open door

ON THE PATH
for my mother

The last breath
of a mother dying
is drawn into a child
being born.
Any child.
This may or
may not
be true.

Tonight
Polaris — diamond
in the black belly
of the great blinding
Mother —
will not let on why

this may or may not
be true.

It must be enough
then
to do only this:
accept from Her
each breath
as if it were your last
as if it were your first.

Breathe true.

WRITER'S BLOCK

Sit beside
a wood fire
all night long
in silent communion
with half a pint
of Southern Comfort

Stumble
at dawn
before the blank paper:
a hunter
numb with the cold

A victim
of buck fever
cursed
condemned
to catch
only a glimpse
of form

stretching across
the page

leaping through
the trees

BIG BSA 650

Willie rides home
on his big BSA 650
with a frightened wife
clinging to his back and
a desperate whisper
in his ear
cutting off the thrust
from bursting up and out
through his pistons and legs
into the soft sweet street
stretched seductively before him —
he holds back
and back
and back
and soon
springs a leak
in his life
leaving him
with a job
a suit and a tie
and the big BSA 650
fading into the back section
of his brown wallet
lumpy
in a backass pocket

GOOFING: CONFESSIONS OF A SHOE STORE MANAGER

from six feet under
my nine-to-five
I find religion

in Apollo's dance
across the parking lot chrome:

He with no time card
to punch
He with no mortgage
due

He lost in the sweet
amber rhythm
of not having
a living soul
to answer to

PRAYER TO THE ROAD KILLS

To those who freeze
before our tons of rolled steel
and prehensile thumbs

To those instinctual followers
of ill-fated paths to home

To those who leave
their intestines to glisten
in our tail light glow

We ask forgiveness

Forgive us
these past 2,000 years
of grafting mind to wheel
of thinking time was ours
    to steal

ICE OUT POEM: A QUARTET

I. Ice In : October, November, December

Night creeps deeper and deeper
into our lives

leaves bleed
throwing themselves
across the darkening waters

the teeth of the pond stir
rising slowly from the mud and stone

the waves, caught by the jugular, still.

II. Ice Here: January, February

Black ice and bright sun, a wisp of snow
carried across the frozen surface. Then
nothing moves but the pond itself

something gurgles and groans beneath my skates
the springs stir in their sleep
beckon to me

I turn away from their tendrils
to glide home

III. Ice Leaving: March, April, May

The heaving begins as
her teeth loosen their grip
Puddles of softening pond shuffle up to the shore. Then
the table turns sending tufts of ice into the
back alley coves.

The outlet gleefully ejaculates.

And the ululating loons return,
testing the water,
choosing to stay for another summer.

IV. Ice Out: June, July, August, September

Whose pond is it, anyways?
The frogs'? The otters'? The heron's?
The dogs' snuffling along the shore?
Certainly the loons could lay claim
returning each year to
grace us with their first born

But of course it's no one's
And never will be

Yet for this one day in August
let us make believe she welcomes us

And we, in turn, grace her with the gift
of our love for one another

and our pledge to keep her
in our hearts

for another year

THREE MEN ON BEMIS MOUNTAIN

A spruce root
bulges out of
thin soil
crosses the trail
then plunges back
into the earth
embracing
I imagine
some subterranean ledge —
no superfluous
leafing or flowering
going on down there —
and yet
"surely this is some
form of intelligence,"
says Al.

I smile
and Bob up ahead
grunts agreement.

We fall back
into
silent
climbing

TO THE TIGER'S LAIR AND BACK
FOR JUDY, GRETCHEN, AND RUTH:
PARO, BHUTAN AND CHESTERVILLE, MAINE
MAY AND JUNE 2012

I.

These sea level lungs
and weary legs
already reeling from a mile plus
altitude adjustment

now climb another mile up
and up

What's the use?
I'll never make it.

> "What's the use?" goes first.
> Then that weird thing called "I"
> that has been trailing this body for years.

The lair is reached.
Two miles above our garden
Ten time zones away.

II.

bending over
pulling yet another rock
from this garden patch
we've tended for three decades
or so
look at the expanse
of weed-cluttered soil
and think

What's the use?
I'll never finish it.

> "What's the use?" goes first.
> Then that pesky "I."

What's left?

Just this.

Just now.

PAEAN TO THE WINTER MOON
ON MY 64TH BIRTHDAY

Most of the time
I keep you in my head
deaf to your silent lullabies
swirling through my blood
numb to your seas
breaking in my kids

Condemned to posing
like Balboa or Cortez
at some ocean's edge

O, leathery sage,
silent midwife
to my cerebral stillbirths,
Forgive me such lunacy

NEW YEAR'S RESOLUTIONS

I resolve
to circle unwarily

to unfold

to make of my life
a gift

to give this gift
to someone I love

to make everyone
someone to love

to do it all over again
and again

until I get it
right

A RETIREMENT CALCULUS
for Judy
June 5, 2013

Each of us
two-thirds of a century
on the planet
two-fifths together

We sit beneath the pergola
late afternoon
watching the wild turkeys scuttle across
the meadow below, head into the tree line,
then back into the tall grass to feed

Our eyes are drawn to the china blue sky
a few wisps of cloud
cross from the north
shape shifting from minute to minute
diminishing and slowly dissolving
slipping into either zero or infinity:
you choose

RETIREMENT POEM

Perhaps we underestimate
the pull of the undertow
along the Florida coast
for the old

Perhaps they seek out hurricanes
only to stand on ion charged beaches
in the most passionate of weather

Perhaps they need to catch the gales full face
feeling their fierce tongues plunging
into their mouths
insistent with the hungry thrust
of lovers long dead

THE BOBCAT TRAIL

Egypt Pond at the end of January, mid afternoon
The sky a bluejay bluish-gray, a light covering of snow
the wind whispering
is the only companion I have
Or need.

I pick up a bobcat's trail, paws running along the edge of the
pond
Follow it to see what happened last night
Then I pick up a human trail, a man's footprints
And begin to follow it. Curiously it parallels the bob cat's

I stop and look back over the pond
Realize that the human trail is mine
From yesterday, I suppose.

Confused for a moment I laugh at my foolishness
Keep moving forward again.

The wind is supposed to pick up tonight
And will probably erase our trails.
No matter. Tomorrow is a new day
The pond an open canvas
Trail free

MIND AS CAR

The clutch is slipping a little
Definitely losing reverse
The rearview mirror is cracked
And I can't remember the last time
I changed the oil

Language creates a metaphysical conundrum:
Is my mind preowned or is it used?
If preowned then what ancient soul
was predestined to stumble into mine?

Better to consider it used:
Radio buttons stuck on the same stations
The backseat jammed with kids laughing
The tires going bald

MIRRORS

I have decided (I think)
that my mind has become a series
of walk-in closets.
You know, the kind with a full length mirror
on the inside of each door.

The door that I just opened
shuts and locks behind me. Looks like
I'm not going back into that room again

But that's okay.
I look into the mirror and see
back over my shoulder
the future swarming into now
my grandchildren approaching, leading my children
my wife, my good friends
the dog
the cat

No, not the cat. She moves out of sight
to lick her paws and wash her face.
She joins the rest of those sentient beings
justifiably uninterested in my eclipsing self-reflections.

CLOSING IN ON OBLIVION: A SONG

I got plenty of hell left to raise
before I'm gone
Still got a place in my heart
for the coming of the dawn
I'm not quite ready to trade in
this life I'm living
Till it's my time to move on
into oblivion

But clichés are starting to come home
to roost
It's getting time to see which truths
are closer to the truth
I'm starting to see what's down the road
from all this living
It's getting time to contemplate
closing in on
oblivion

Still I can't quite get my head around
There'll be no more need
to stand my ground
No more "me" no more "I" to
chase on down
Not when I'm closing in
on oblivion

But when the siren song
of nonexistence
gets to humming in the air
And it becomes so irrefutably,
so perfectly clear,
that all my roads have been travelled
and all my bells have been rung
Then I'll open up my heart
and my soul
to sweet sweet
oblivion

PRELUDE TO AN EPITAPH

Wait!
Where was I?
Ah, yes.

EPITAPH

12:31pm
Friday
at last

STONE FENCE

If I lay here long enough
in this early Spring sun
perhaps I'll become

as free as the wood snake
come here to shed her skin

Or better yet
become the wall itself:

my bones into resolute stone

my voice dead leaves
caught in patterned crevasses

my mind moss
seeping slowly down

into a forgiving earth

COMING TO THE END
LACONIA, NEW HAMPSHIRE WINTER 2014

the night surrounds me
with its lack of constant sound:
an occasional car winking by
a cat settling into
the corner chair

I am finally approaching
absolute silence

brought to a point
of no return

a body becoming
what it always was fated to be:

grid of bone and gristle
spreading slowly outward —
connecting tissue snapping
free in the breeze

like prayer flags
laid out
by the Bhutanese

ORION RISING

III. FIDDLEHEADS:

POEMS FOR CHILDREN

III. FIDDLEHEADS: POEMS FOR CHILDREN

Published in 1982 for my kids and their friends. The original edition included eighteen poems with illustrations by Martha Lively.

I found writing children's poems to be both exhilarating and challenging. I wrote most of these during the time Josh and Jen were about five and seven, respectively. We were deeply immersed in A.A. Milne, caught up in his poems' musicality and utter joy of language play.

Much like taking a walk with a small child, and letting her or him "lead," I carried this musicality into the woods and meadows and followed it where it may. I tried to capture for myself and them the sheer joy of wonder and play in the fields of whatever Creative Force we choose to worship.

FIDDLEHEADS

Wondering out loud
one day
in a very special way
I wondered at this:
When I open up
my hand
what happens to
my fist?

Just then
in reply
a butterfly
all yellow, green,
and sunset red
brushed by
telling me
of the fiddleheads
marching up
from the meadow
each spring
just to carry down

past the woodchuck town
a year's supply
of forgotten fists,
turning each
as they go
into daffodils
buttercups
and daisies as white
as snow

RAINBOW GIRL

What a strange little girl
said all the doctors
(and the nurses too)

Her throat is yellow
and her belly button's blue

and look! her knees are
a bright summer green!

What could it be?
Is she sick or
possibly in pain?

Oh no,
not all or
any of that:

she just drank up
a hatful of rain

and gobbled down
a most enormous chunk
of sunbeam
(which I suppose
made her mouth
feel sunny)

So of course
she's all those colors!

Wouldn't you be
with a rainbow
in your tummy?

TOPSY

What should we do
with that little girl
who sticks her toes
up her nose

turning herself
into a wheel
that rolls and rolls

who loses her
red, white and green
bows and bows and bows?

Why I suppose
we should ask her
quite sternly
to stop

and turn herself back
into a
more respectable
topsy-turvy
top.

VEGETARIAN DOUBTS

Since animals
are my pals,
I don't eat meat

Day and night
I pack
those veggies in
good and tight

But suppose
I end up
with a zucchini
for a nose?

Or carrots
for ears?

Maybe onions
would roll down
my cheeks
instead of tears

and parsley would grow
where my fingers
should be

And what if
every time I'd try
to talk
out would come
a celery stalk?

Oh, I know
vegetables
will sharpen my eyes
and improve my hearing

but sometimes
I really do doubt
if I like being
a vegetarian!

ODE TO OATMEAL

Every winter morning
my mommy wants me
to eat my oatmeal
(and daddy does too) —
Me?
I would just as soon
eat a pot of glue!

Oh, they cut up the dates
and plop in a few raisins
but it still tastes
like some yucky old paste

So, when they're not looking
when something else is cooking
I slip my bowl under my chair
and feed it to my good old teddy bear

And you know what?
He doesn't say a thing
taking it all in
without even a sigh

but the poor guy
I can't help wondering
what he must look inside

SEARCHING FOR CEDAR

Marching in the morning rain
up through the pucker brush
we came:
a squiggly line of adventurous
yellow, red, blue, and green
country slickers

Up we went
into the grove
of the lordly cedars
into
the cathedral silence

of cedar needles

FLOWER SONG

Live your life
like a flower

Blossoming every hour

Reaching for the sun

Growing with the rain

Living every moment
like it'll never come again

SPRING SINGING

Time to sing
with the newborn grasses
the giggling crocuses

Time to hop
with the robins
snatching up their breakfasts

Time to follow
barn swallows
skimming on by

Time to close eyes
and be wings
and morning song

singing Spring

soaring up
into the sun.

SIX MOON TUNES

1.

moon
is a friend
in the forest
lending me
her light
on what would
otherwise be
a most
dreadfully dark
and spooky
night

2.

on hot,
smothering
suffocating
summer nights
(when everything
moves
at its very
slowest speed)
moon makes
a wonderful
target
for a cool
and slippery
watermelon seed

3.

when the world
looks so sad
gloomy
and unespecially
dull
there's nothing
quite like
the brightest
whitest
widest
smile
of moon
when she's
balloony full

SIX MOON TUNES

4.

sometimes
when it seems like
winter is here to stay
it's a happy
hip! hip! hooray!
kind of night
dressing up all
bundily warm
and snuggily tight
for a run down
to the meadow
to dance and dance
with my very own
moon shadow

5.

I'm very certain
old moon
is well acquainted
with our dopey dog
(and mr. owl too)
staying up
all night long
as they often do
singing their own
special
howly
hooty
sing-along song

6.

but he or she
(as the case may be)
all full up
to the brim
or thin
as a sliver
is still
my best bedtime
buddy
whispering to me
ever so softly
her green-cheesy secrets
which I can never quite remember

GRAVITY EXPERIMENT
to the two Joshes

We all know
that octopi
don't fly
And neither do
kangaroo.
But what if we took
a moose
and pumped
his antlers
full of air
and then cut him
loose —
what do you suppose
he would do?

Probably
just stand there
and stare
at such a silly goose
as you
trying to shoot him —
merely a moose —
full of air
while he's very satisfied
(thank you very much)
to munch on a bush
while philosophizing upon
the glorious sound
that four hooves can make
when they are securely planted
on solid ground.

MANIFESTO FOR JOSH

Grab a flake
of now
swirling
all about you

lay down
and let it melt
into your childheart

reach out
and let it wash
over you

stand still
and let it cover
your tracks

move on
and feel no regrets
at the closing
of the day.

JEN

The birch splits
its bark
the snake its skin
the child leaps
into the woman
she always has been

Nothing is new
nothing is changing
the birch is the bark
the snake the skin
the child the woman

The seed, flowering,
dies back into the earth
as the child, growing,
turns forward toward
her new birth

EPILOGUE

DAD'S SONG

Sit beside me
and we'll
sing along
with
the meadows
the swallows
and the stone wall:

you and me
under the tree

backs to the wall

watching the swallows
be.

Index of First Lines